Simply Mus...

The Best Songs from Broadway

18 Popular Melodies

Arranged by Dan Coates

Simply Musicals is a collection of hits from the greatest musicals, both past and present. These songs have been carefully selected and arranged by Dan Coates for Easy Piano, making them accessible to pianists of all ages. Phrase markings, articulations, fingering, pedaling, and dynamics have been included to aid with interpretation, and a large print size makes the notation easy to read.

From elementary school productions to sold-out Broadway shows, people have fallen in love with the songs from musicals. Classic shows keep finding new generations of fans. Young performers delight in singing "Try to Remember" from *The Fantasticks*, while the sparkle of "The Gold Diggers' Song (We're in the Money)" from *42nd Street* continues to charm audiences. New hit shows prove that talented composers and lyricists are still hard at work. The pop/rock musicals *Spring Awakening* and *American Idiot* have expanded the genre of the musical and opened up Broadway to a new audience.

With their ability to make us laugh and cry, musicals have been embraced by musicians and audiences, young and old, around the world. For these reasons and more, the following pages are exciting to explore.

After all, this is *Simply Musicals!*

Produced by
Alfred Music Publishing Co., Inc.
P.O. Box 10003
Van Nuys, CA 91410-0003
alfred.com

ISBN-10: 0-7390-6714-1
ISBN-13: 978-0-7390-6714-7

Cover Photo
© istockphoto / DNY59

Contents

Chitty Chitty Bang Bang
(from "Chitty Chitty Bang Bang")

Words and Music by
Richard M. Sherman and Robert B. Sherman
Arranged by Dan Coates

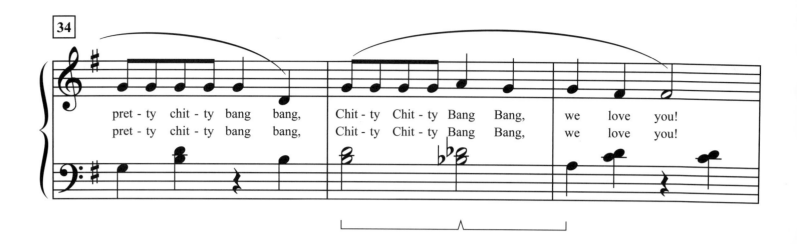

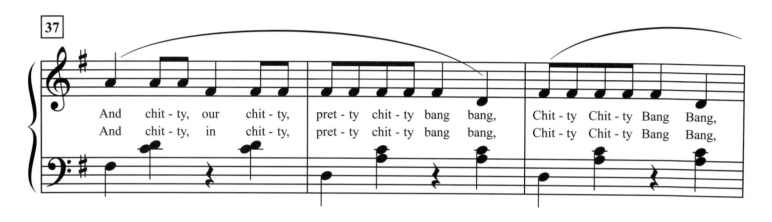

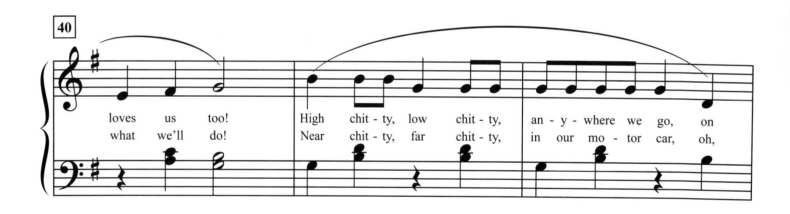

8

21 Guns
(from "American Idiot")

Lyrics by Billie Joe
Music by Green Day
Arranged by Dan Coates

Aquarius
(from "Hair")

Lyrics by James Rado and Gerome Ragni
Music by Galt MacDermot
Arranged by Dan Coates

Can You Feel the Love Tonight

(From Walt Disney's "The Lion King")

Music by Elton John
Words by Tim Rice
Arranged by Dan Coates

Moderately slow ballad

1. There's a calm_ sur-ren-der to the rush_ of day,
2. There's a time_ for ev-'ry-one, if they on-ly learn

best.

mp

It's e - nough___ to make kings___ and vag - a - bonds___ be -

lieve the ver - y best.

rit. e dim.

p

Corner of the Sky
(from "Pippin")

Music and Lyrics by Stephen Schwartz
Arranged by Dan Coates

Brightly, with a steady rhythm

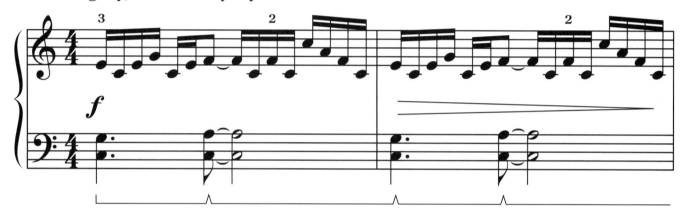

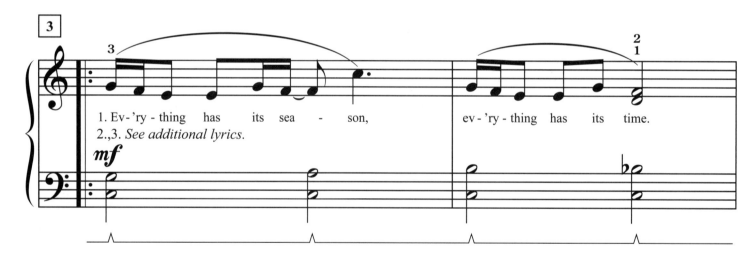

1. Ev-'ry-thing has its sea - son, ev-'ry-thing has its time.
2.,3. *See additional lyrics.*

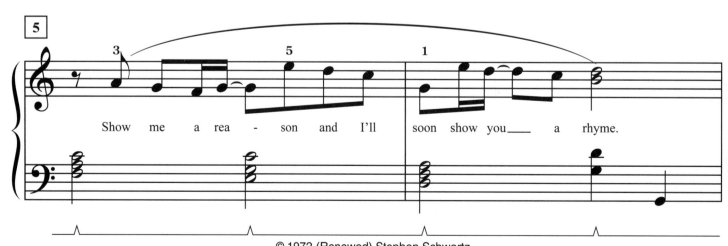

Show me a rea - son and I'll soon show you____ a rhyme.

Cats fit on the win - dow sill, chil - dren fit in the snow.___

Why do I feel I___ don't fit in an - y - where___ I go?

Riv - ers be - long where they can ram - ble,

ea - gles be - long where they can soar.

simile

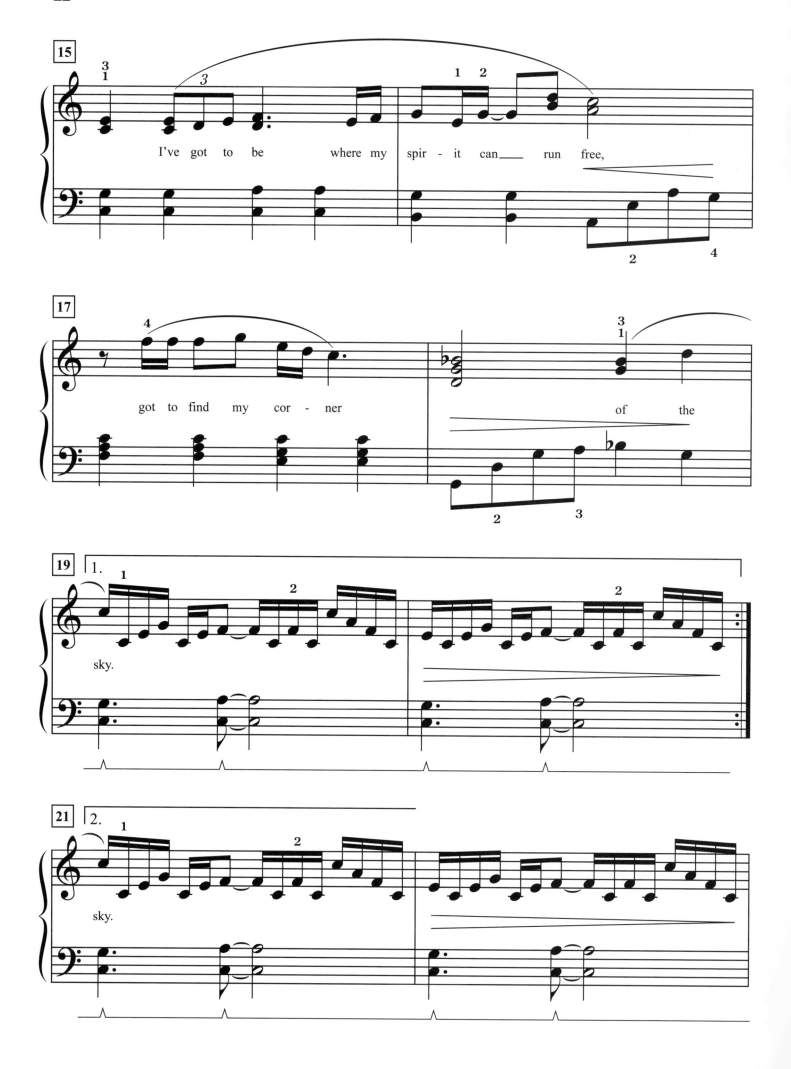

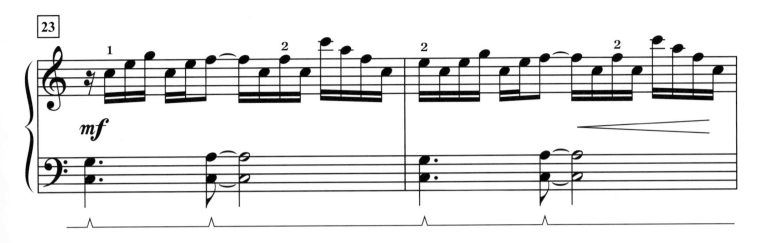

Verse 2:
Every man has his daydreams,
Every man has his goals.
People like the way dreams have of
Sticking to the soul.
Thunderclouds have their lightning,
Nightingales have their song,
And don't you see I want my life to be
Something more than long?
(To Chorus:)

Verse 3:
So many men seemed destined
To settle for something small.
But I won't rest until I
Know I'll have it all.
So, don't ask where I'm going,
Just listen when I'm gone.
And, far away, you'll hear me singing
Softly to the dawn.
(To Chorus:)

Falling In Love with Love
(from "The Boys from Syracuse")

Words by Lorenz Hart
Music by Richard Rodgers
Arranged by Dan Coates

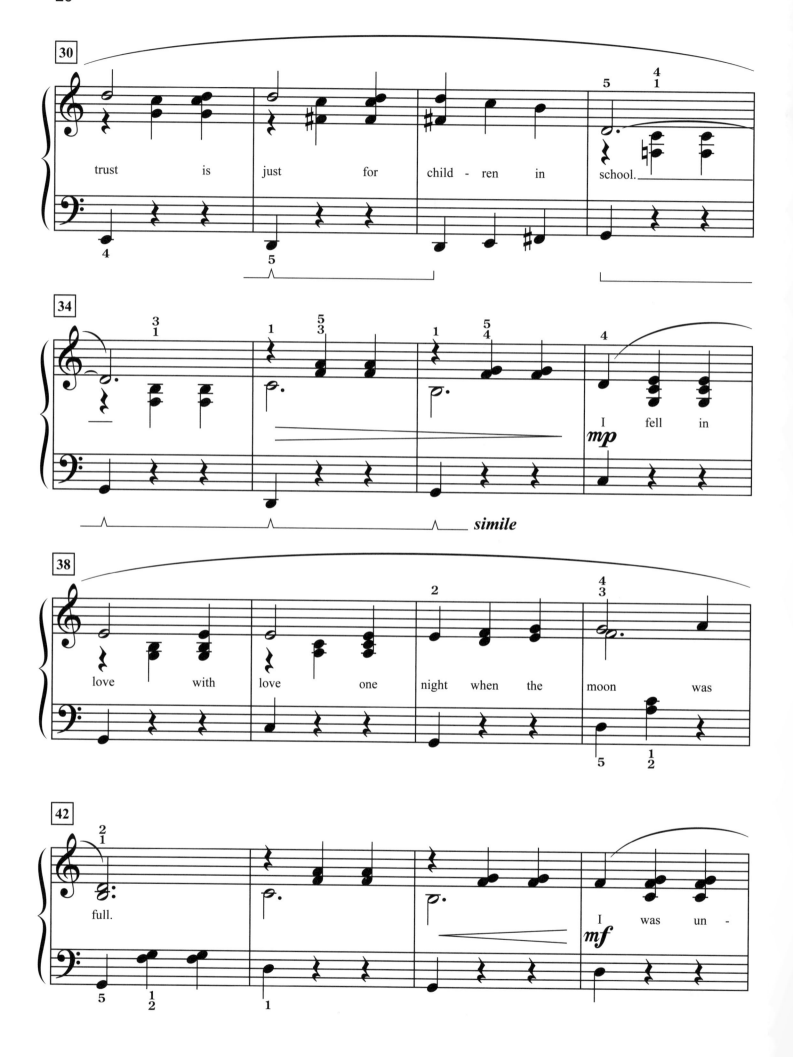

trust   is   just   for   child - ren   in   school. _____

I   fell   in

love   with   love   one   night   when   the   moon   was

full.

I   was   un -

Give My Regards to Broadway
(WWI Version)
(from "Little Johnny Jones")

Words and Music by George M. Cohan
Arranged by Dan Coates

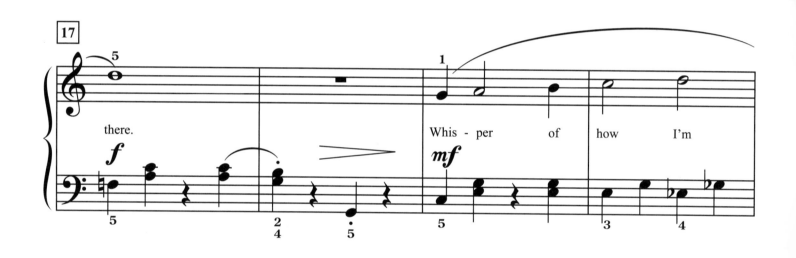

throng. _____ Give my re - gards to

old Broad - way and say that I'll be there e'er

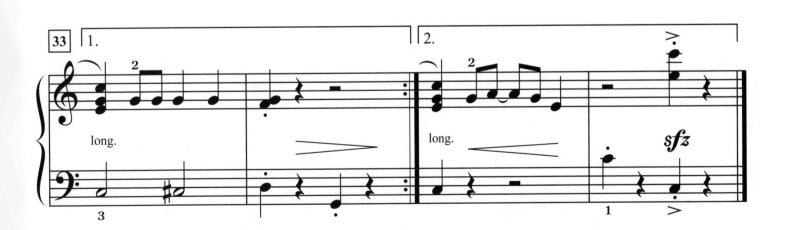

long. long.

The Gold Diggers' Song
(We're in the Money)

(from "42nd Street")

Lyrics by Al Dubin
Music by Harry Warren
Arranged by Dan Coates

Mama Who Bore Me
(from "Spring Awakening")

Lyrics by Steven Sater
Music by Duncan Sheik
Arranged by Dan Coates

Christ will come___ a' call - ing. They light a can - dle and hope that it glows.

And some just lie there, cry-ing for Him to come and find them. But when He come, they don't know how to

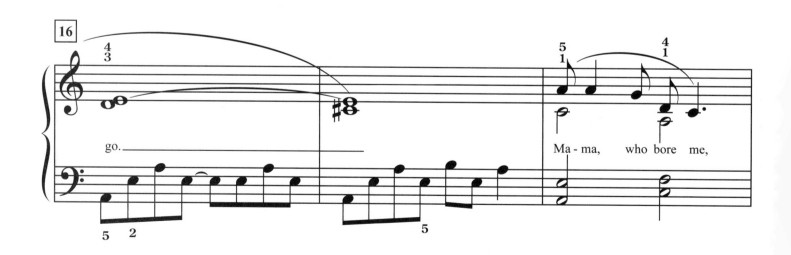

go.___ Ma - ma, who bore me,

Ma - ma, who gave me no way to han - dle things, who made me so bad.

Ma - ma, the weep - ing, Ma - ma, the an - gels. No sleep in Heav - en

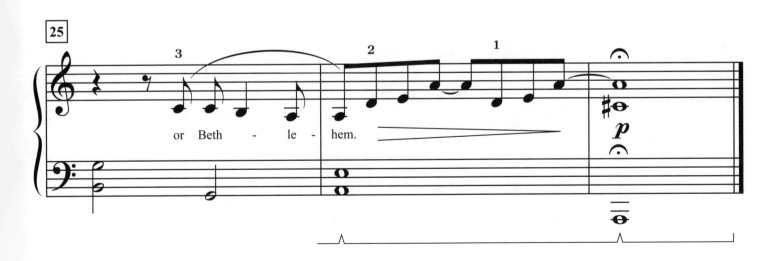

or Beth - le - hem.

How Lucky You Are
(from "Seussical the Musical")

Lyrics by Lynn Ahrens
Music by Stephen Flaherty
Arranged by Dan Coates

When the news is all bad,— when you're sour— and blue,— when you

start to get mad,— you should do— what I do:

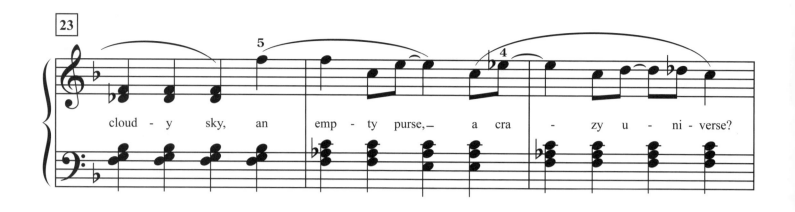

cloud-y sky, an emp-ty purse,— a cra - zy u - ni - verse?

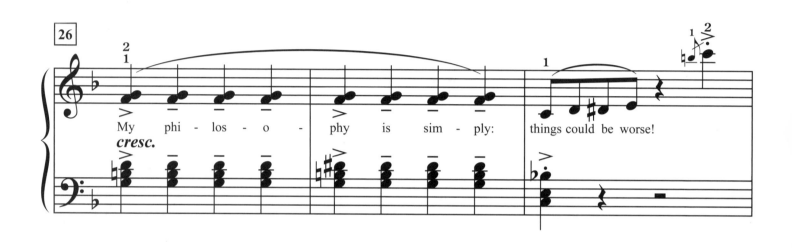

My phi-los-o-phy is sim-ply: things could be worse!

So be hap-py you're here.— Think of life as a thrill!— And if

worse comes to worse— (as we all— know it will), thank your luck-y star—

you've got-ten this far.
And

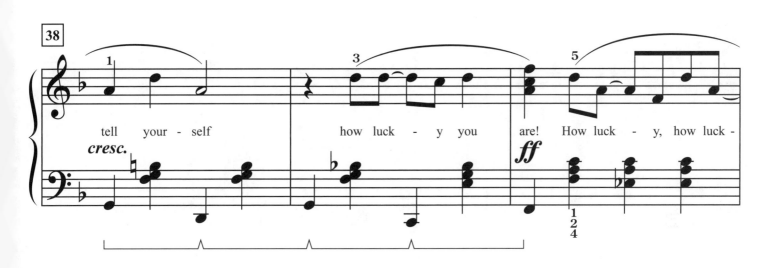

tell your-self
cresc.
how luck - y you
are! How luck - y, how luck -

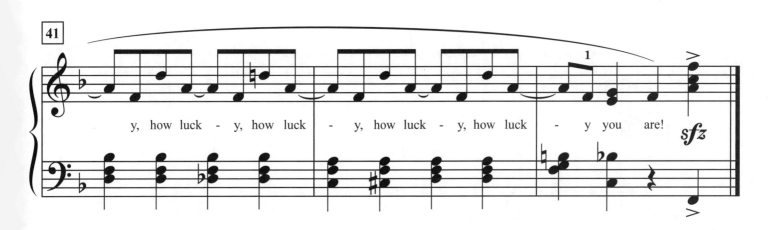

y, how luck - y, how luck - y, how luck-y, how luck - y you are!
sfz

It's My Party
(from "The Marvelous Wonderettes")

Words and Music by
Herb Wiener, John Gluck and Wally Gold
Arranged by Dan Coates

Moderately bright

The Knights of the Round Table

(from "Spamalot")

Music by Neil Innes
Lyrics by John Cleese and Graham Chapman
Arranged by Dan Coates

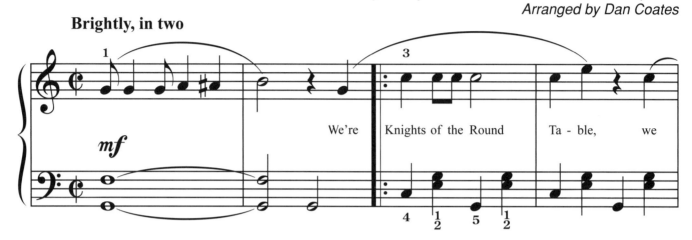

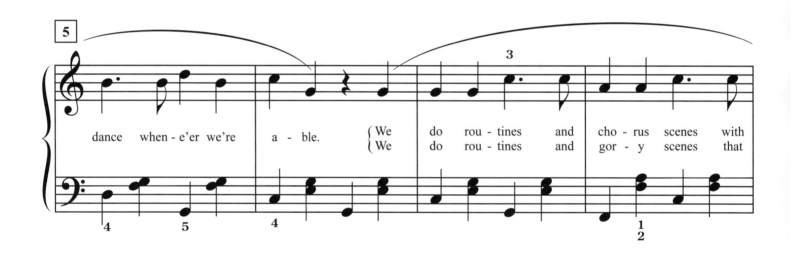

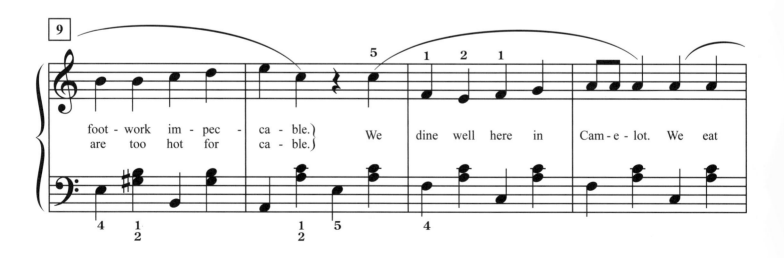

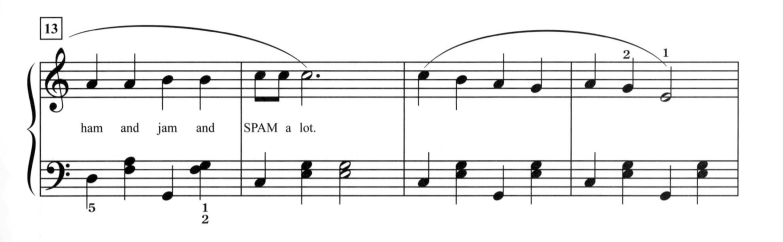

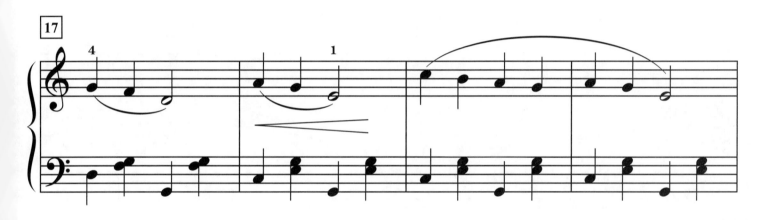

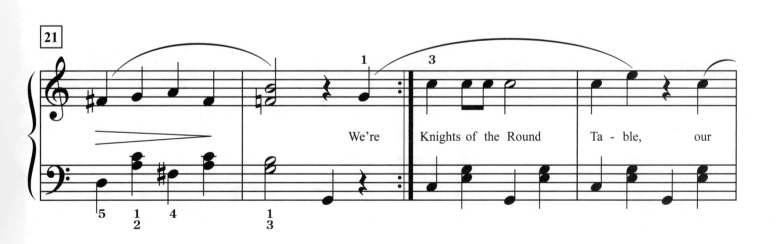

shows are for - mid - a - ble. But, man - y times we're giv - en rhymes that

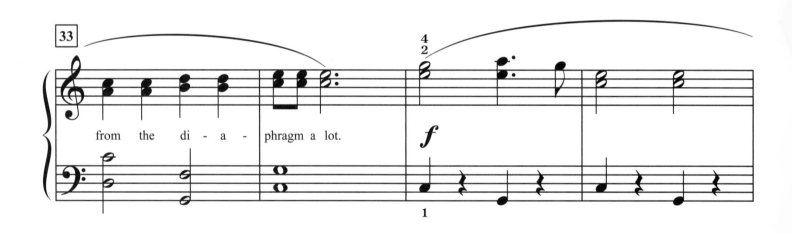

are quite un - sing - a - ble. We're op - era - mad in Cam - e - lot. We sing

from the di - a - phragm a lot. *f*

We're Knights of the Round Ta - ble, al -

mf

Part of Your World
(from Walt Disney's "The Little Mermaid")

Music by Alan Menken
Lyrics by Howard Ashman
Arranged by Dan Coates

stand.   Bet they don't   re - pri - mand their   daugh - ters.   Bright young

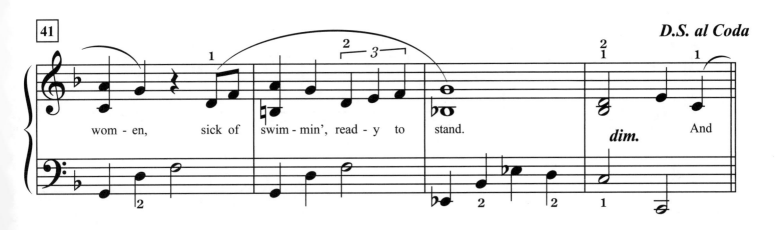

D.S. al Coda

wom - en,   sick of   swim - min', read - y   to   stand.   *dim.*   And

Coda

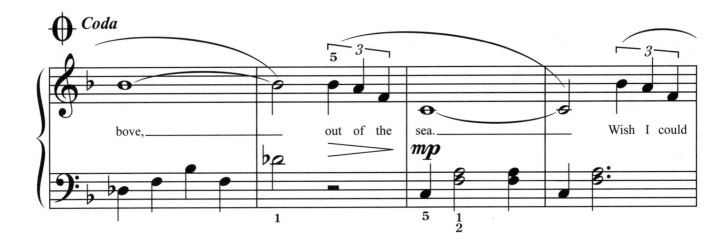

bove,_____   out of the   sea._____   Wish I could

mp

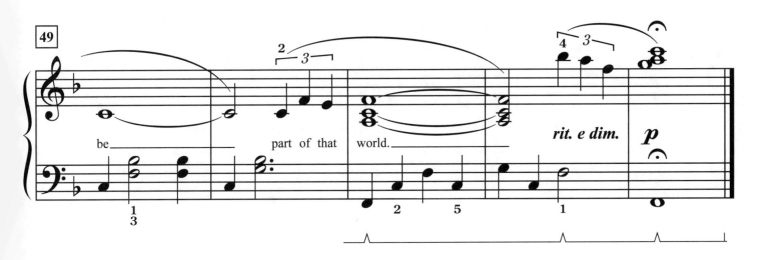

be_____   part of that   world._____   *rit. e dim.*   *p*

Suddenly Seymour
(from "Little Shop of Horrors")

Words by Howard Ashman
Music by Alan Menken
Arranged by Dan Coates

Moderately slow, in 2

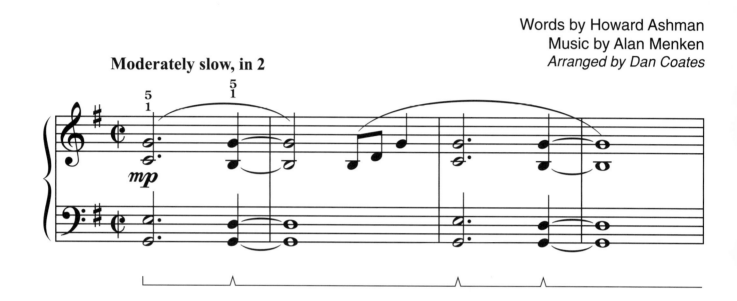

Lift up your head.___ Wash off your mas-ca - ra.

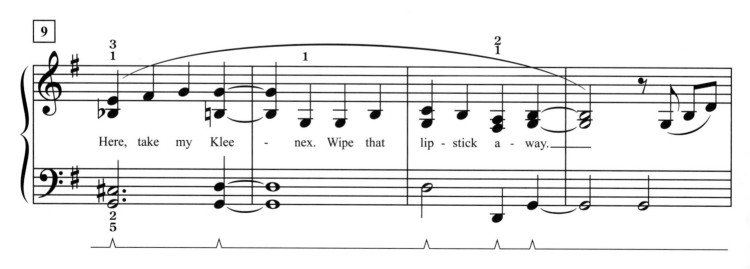

Here, take my Klee - nex. Wipe that lip - stick a - way.___

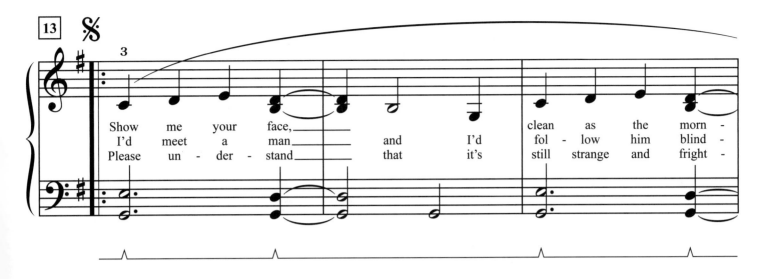

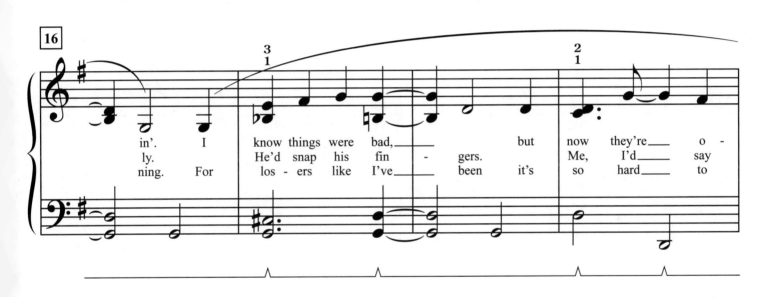

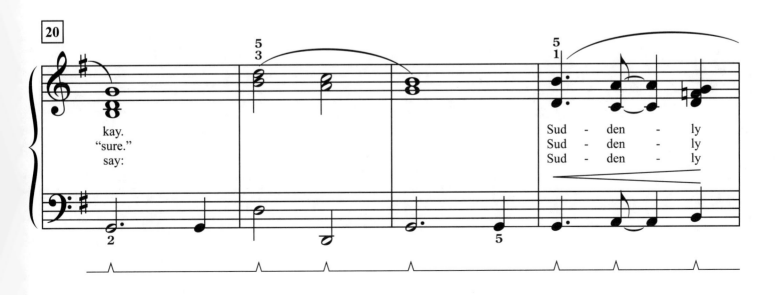

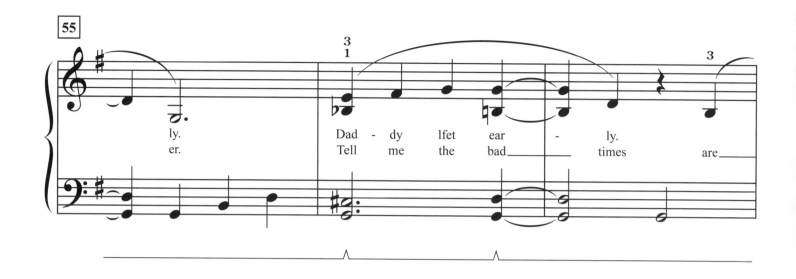

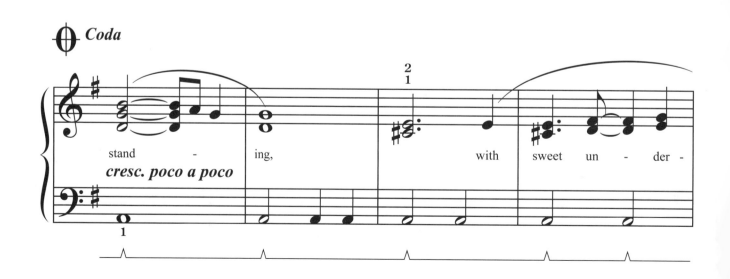

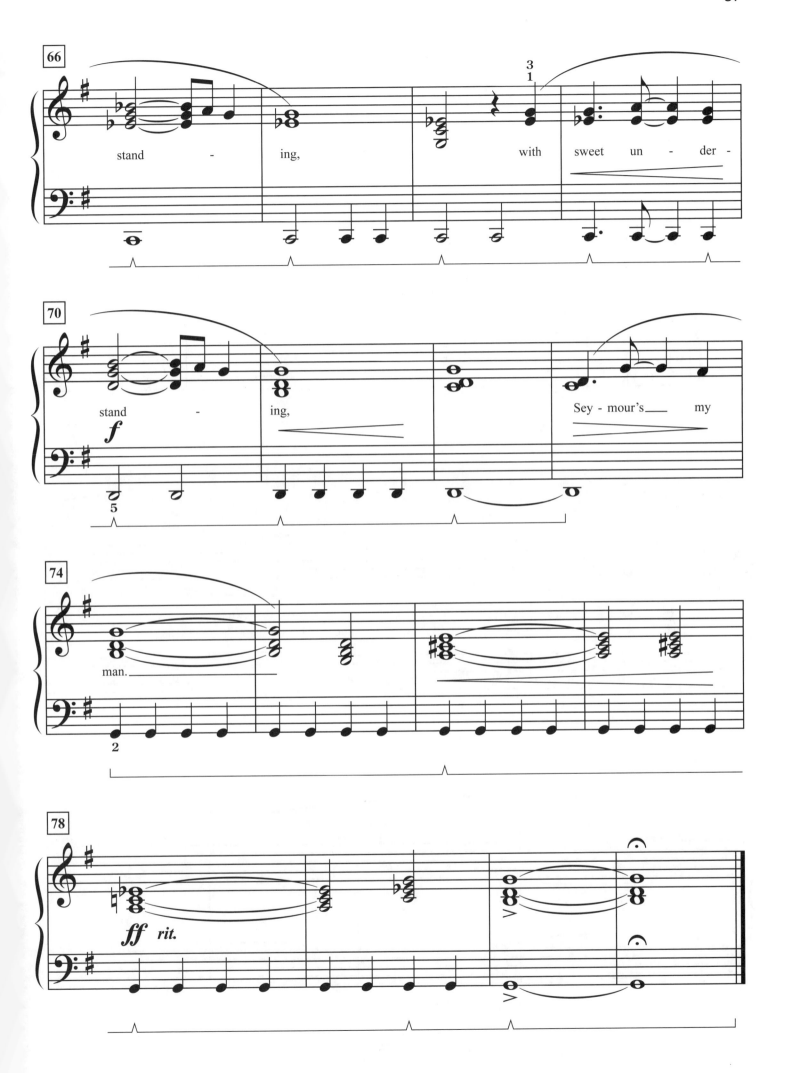

Tenterfield Saddler
(from "The Boys of Oz")

By Peter Woolnough Allen
Arranged by Dan Coates

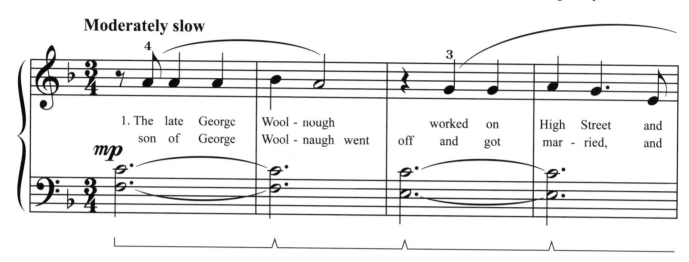

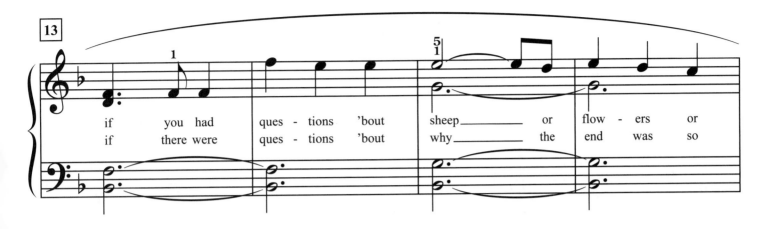

if you had ques - tions 'bout sheep_____ or flow - ers or
if there were ques - tions 'bout why_____ the end was so

dogs,_____ you'd just ask the
sad,_____ well, George had no

Sad - dler._____ He lived with - out sin; they're
an - swers_____ a - bout why a son

60

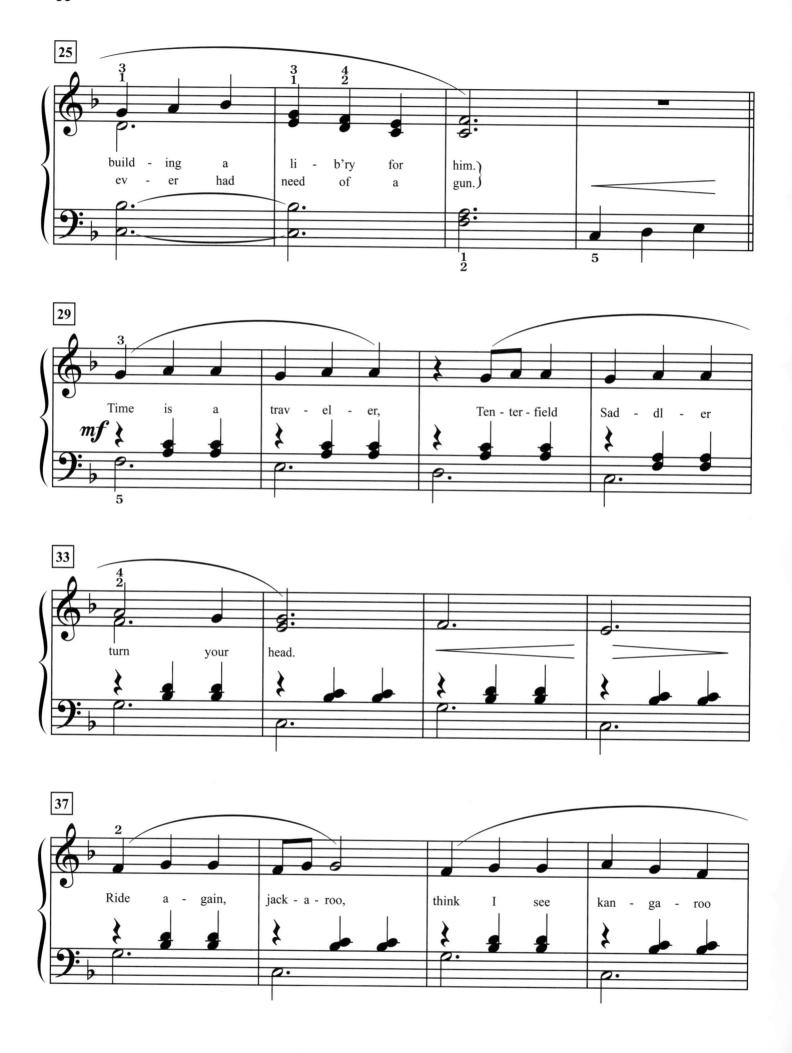

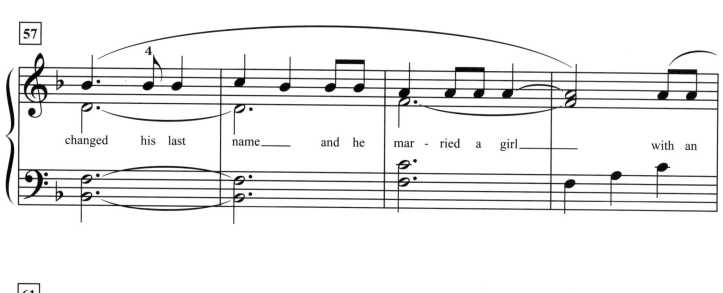

changed his last name___ and he mar - ried a girl___ ___ with an

in - t'rest - ing face. He'd

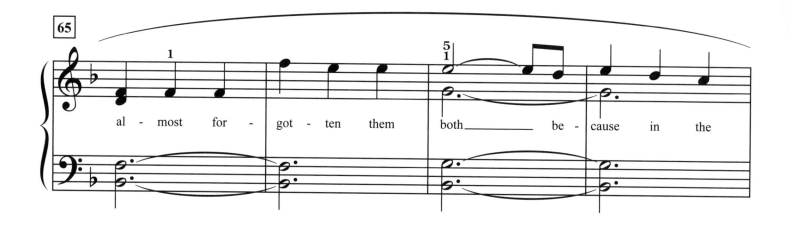

al - most for - got - ten them both___ ___ be - cause in the

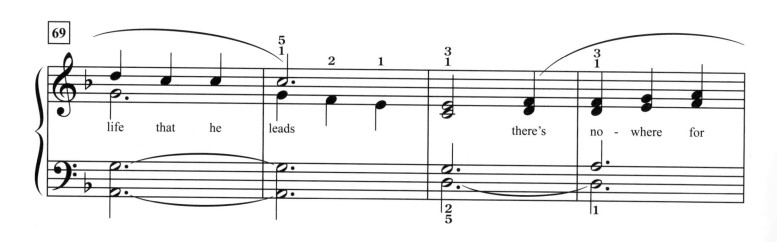

life that he leads there's no - where for

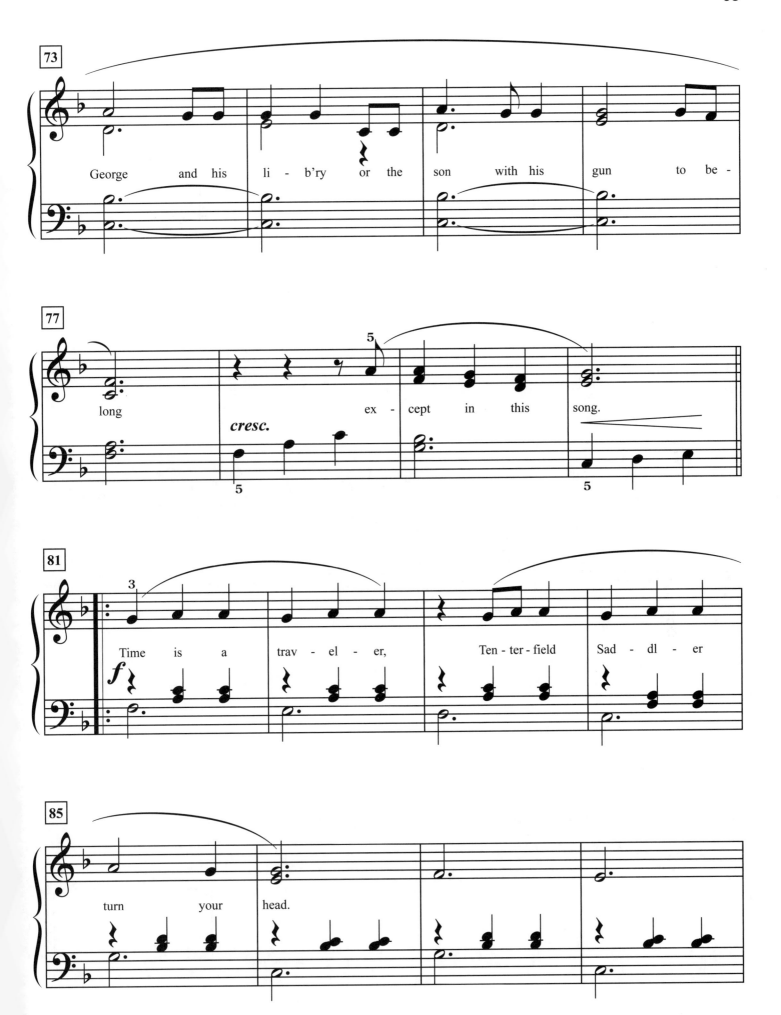

George and his li - b'ry or the son with his gun to be -

long except in this song.

cresc.

Time is a trav - el - er, Ten - ter - field Sad - dl - er

turn your head.

Ride a - gain, jack - a - roo, think I see kan - ga - roo

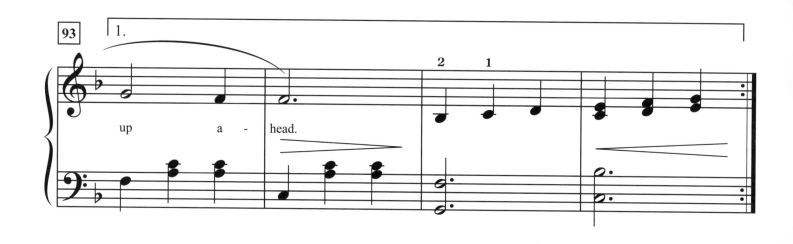

1.

up a - head.

2.

up a - head.

rit. e dim.

mf

Try to Remember
(from "The Fantasticks")

Lyrics by Tom Jones
Music by Harvey Schmidt
Arranged by Dan Coates

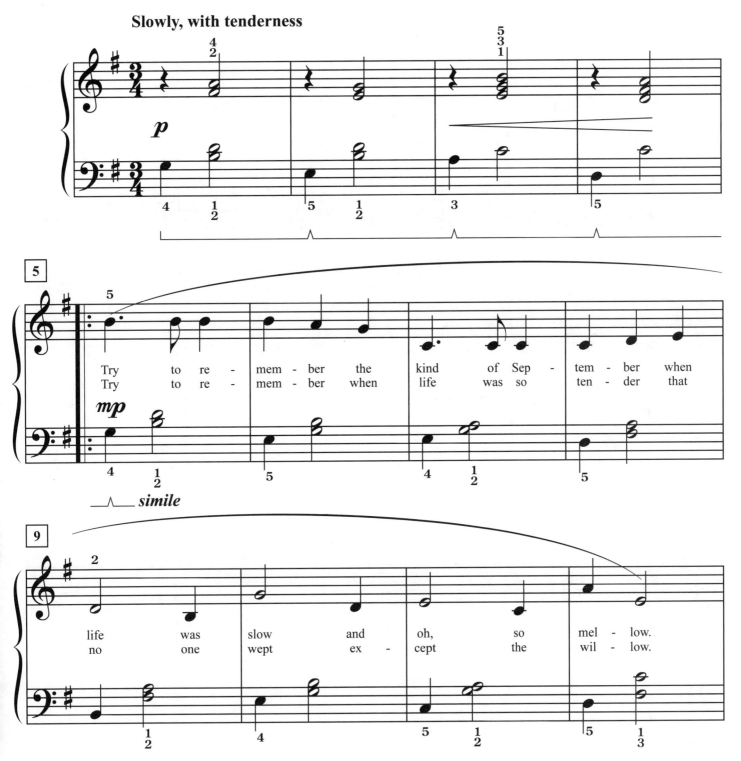

What More Can I Say?

(from "The Falsettos")

Words and Music by William Finn
Arranged by Dan Coates

Moderate ballad

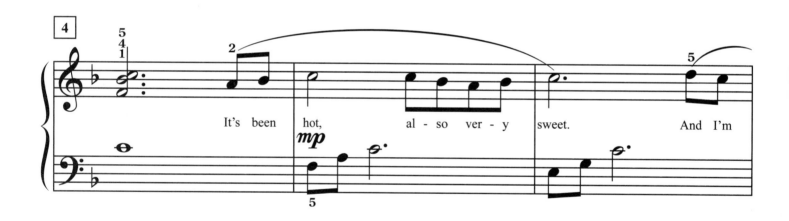

It's been hot, al - so ver - y sweet. And I'm

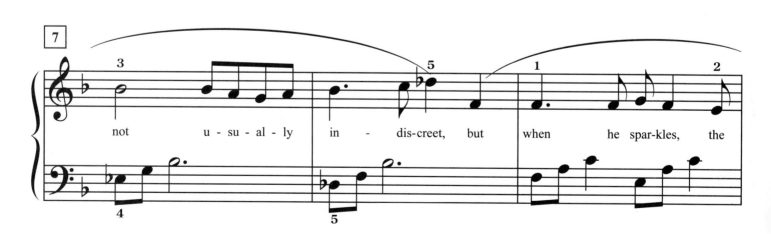

not u - su - al - ly in - dis-creet, but when he spar-kles, the

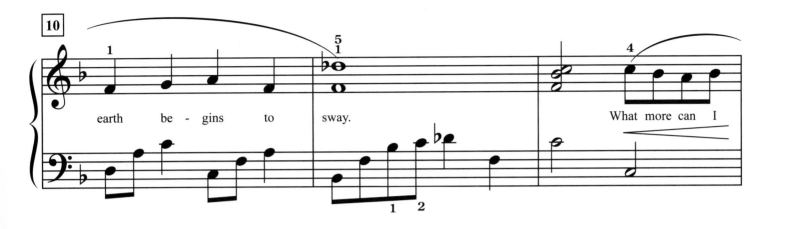

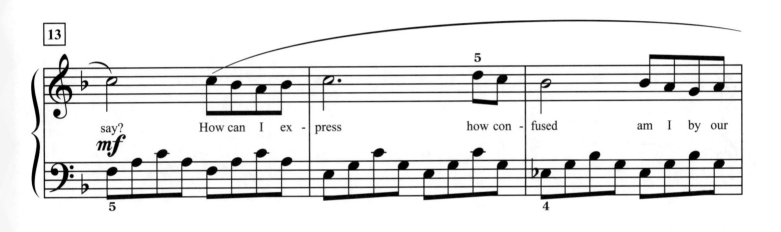

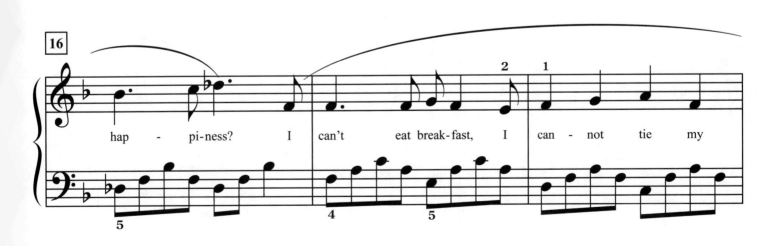

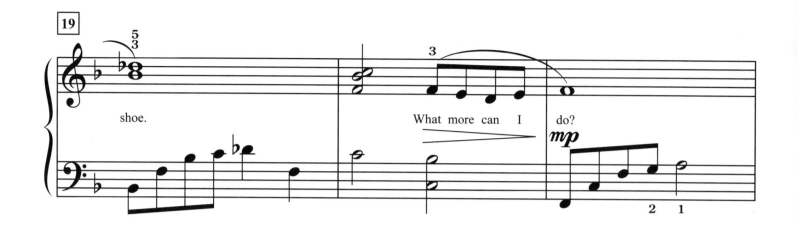

shoe.

What more can I do?

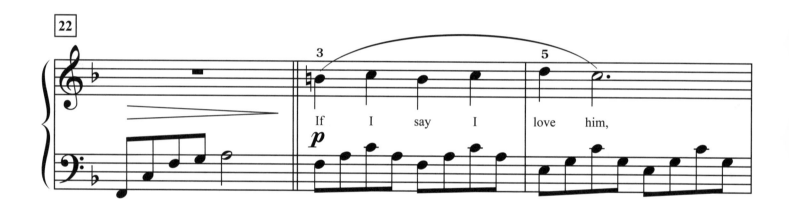

If I say I love him,

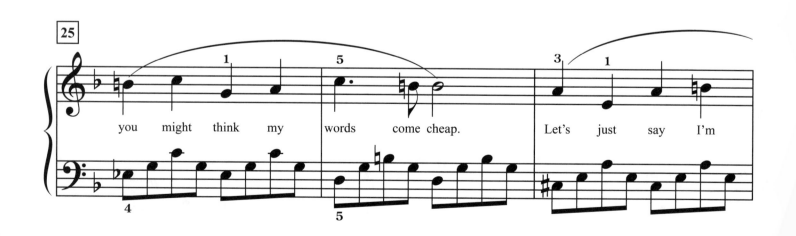

you might think my words come cheap. Let's just say I'm

28

glad he's mine, a - wake, a - sleep. It's been

mp

31

hot, al - so ver - y swell. More than not, it's been more than
taught: nev - er brag or shout. Still it's hot, just like how you

mp

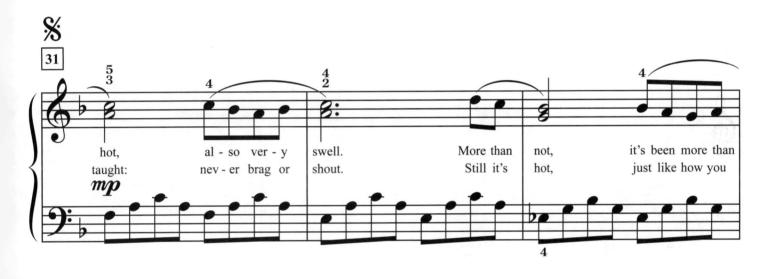

34

words can tell. I halt, I stam - mer, I sing a ron - de -
read a - bout. And al - so car - ing and nev - er too un -

The Winner Takes It All
(from "Mamma Mia!")

Words and Music by
Benny Andersson and Bjorn Ulvaeus
Arranged by Dan Coates

75

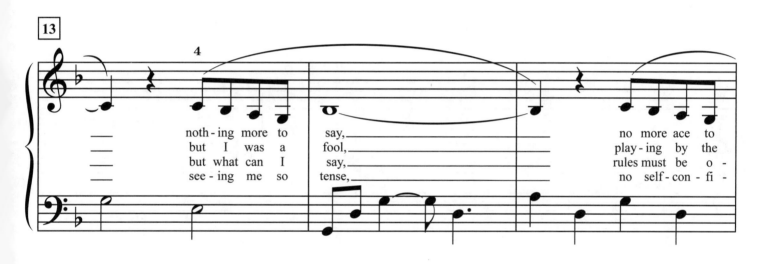

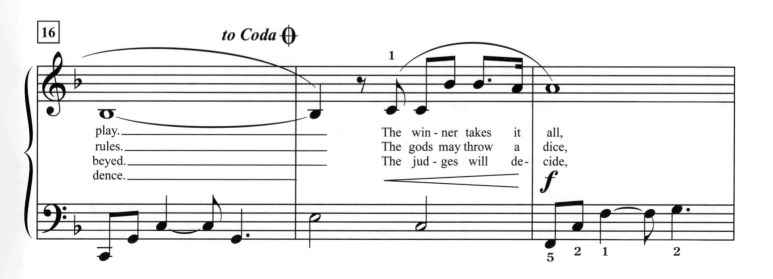

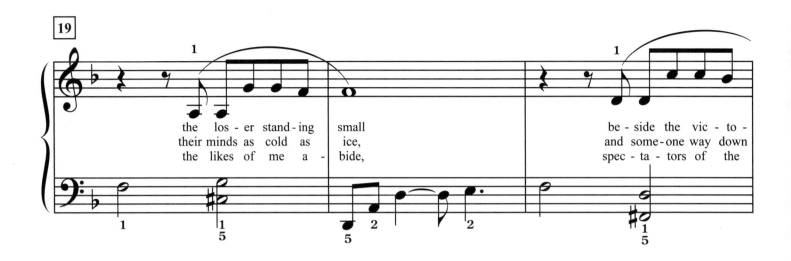

the los - er stand - ing small
their minds as cold as ice,
the likes of me a - bide,

be - side the vic - to -
and some - one way down
spec - ta - tors of the

ry,
here
show,

that's her des - ti - ny.
los - es some - one dear.
al - ways stay - ing low.

1.

2., 3.

2. I was in your

The win - ner takes it all,
The game is on a - gain,

the los - er has to fall,
a lov - er or a friend,

it's sim - ple and it's
a big thing or a

plain,_____
small,_____

why should I com - plain?
the win - ner takes it all._____

D.S. al Coda

1.

3. But tell me does she

2.

4. I don't wan - na

the win-ner takes it all.

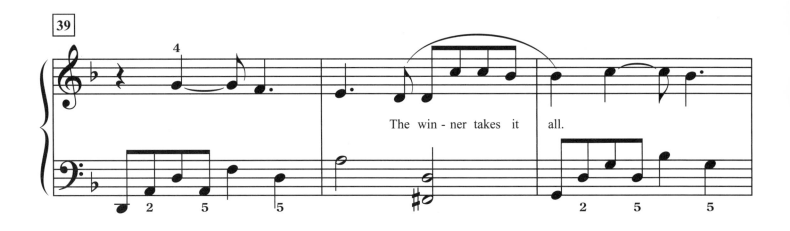

The win-ner takes it all.

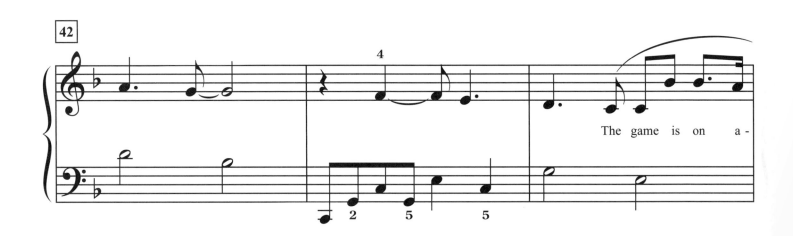

The game is on a-

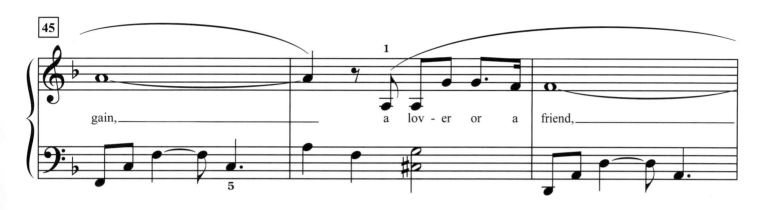

gain,_____ a lov - er or a friend,_____

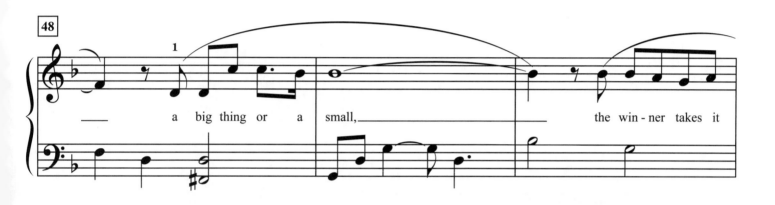

____ a big thing or a small,_____ the win - ner takes it

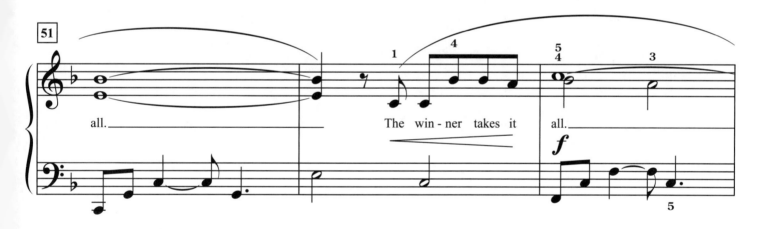

all._____ The win - ner takes it all._____

f

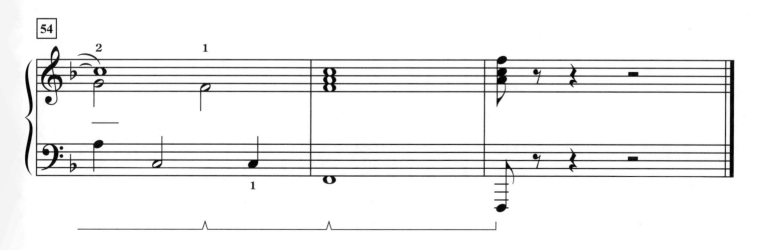